The Lord works marvels for me.
Holy is his name.

The Beautiful Story of Mary

Text and illustrations: Maïte Roche

CTS Children's Books

The Beautiful Story of Mary: Published 2011 by the Incorporated Catholic Truth Society, 40-46 Harleyford Road, London SE11 5AY. Tel: 020 7640 0042; Fax: 020 7640 0046; www.cts-online.org.uk. Copyright © 2011 The Incorporated Catholic Truth Society in this English-language edition.

ISBN: 978 1 86082 762 4   CTS Code CH 37

Translated from the French Edition by Helena Scott: **La belle histoire de Marie** written and illustrated by Maïte Roche, published 2010 by Edifa-Mame, 15-27 rue Moussorgski, 75018 Paris; ISBN Mame 978-2-7289-1356-5; Edifa 978-2-9163-5071-4; Copyright © Mame-Édifa - 2010.

Maïte Roche

The Beautiful Story of Mary

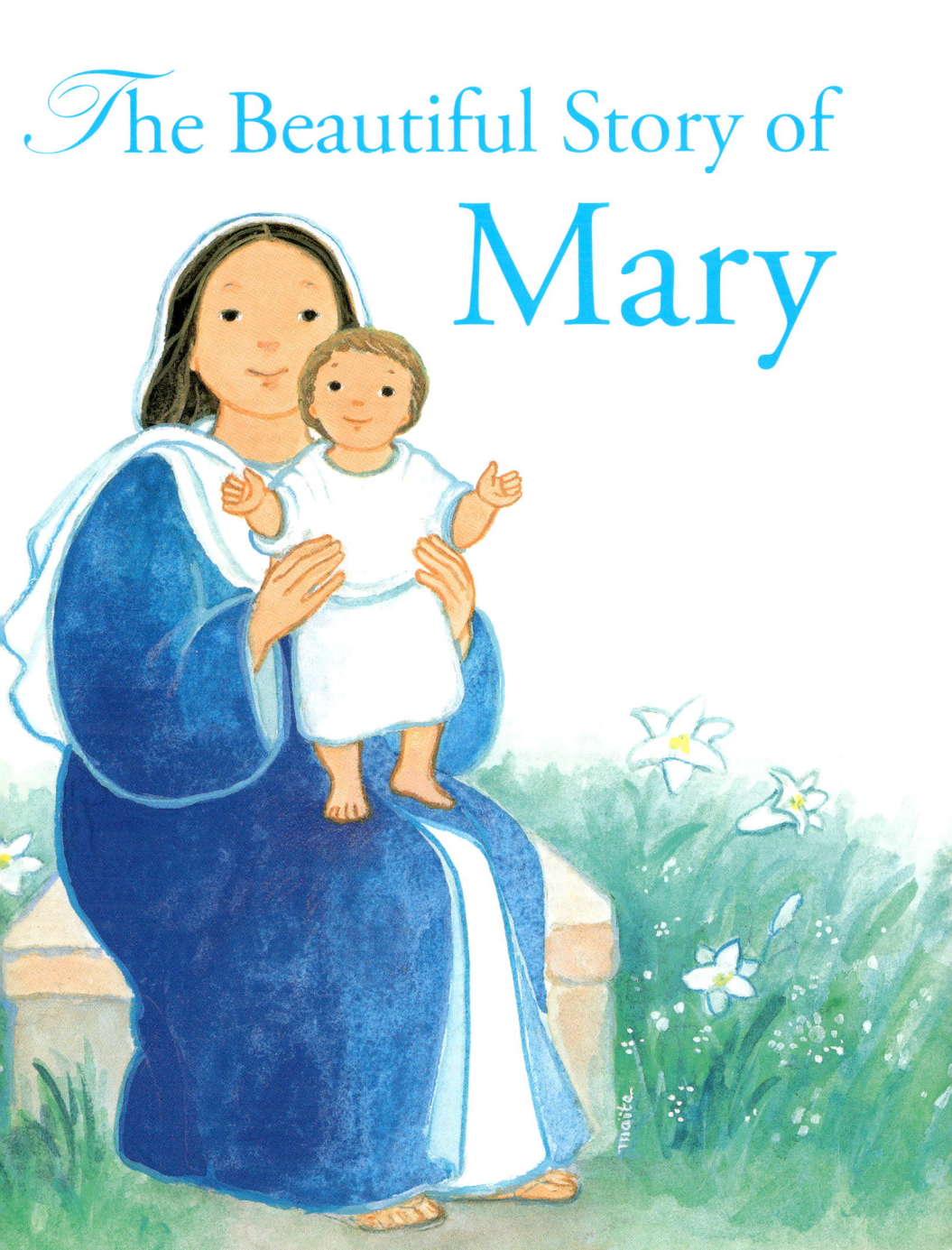

Mary was born in Nazareth, a little village in Galilee. From the very beginning of her life, the grace of God had been with her. Her Mummy, Anne, and her Daddy, Joachim, blessed the Lord every day and thanked Him for His love. Mary learned to know and love God with all her heart, and, like her parents, she waited for the Saviour who would bring happiness.

Mary was growing up. She was always ready to help her Mummy. She wove material for clothes, she went to the spring to fetch water, and she cooked the meals. Joseph, her fiancé, was a carpenter. He was a descendent of the family of King David. Like Mary, he was good and honest, and he loved serving God.

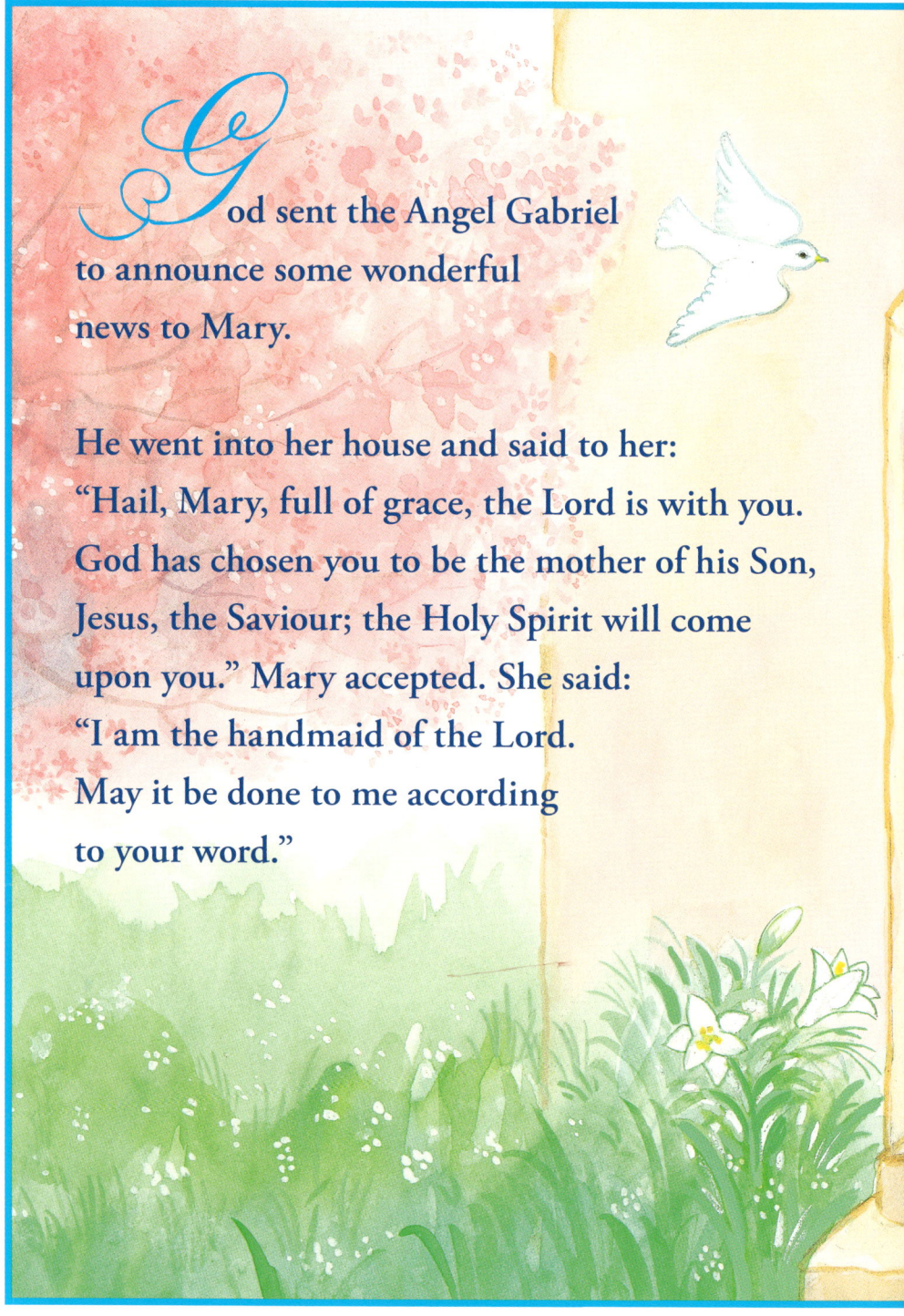

God sent the Angel Gabriel to announce some wonderful news to Mary.

He went into her house and said to her: "Hail, Mary, full of grace, the Lord is with you. God has chosen you to be the mother of his Son, Jesus, the Saviour; the Holy Spirit will come upon you." Mary accepted. She said: "I am the handmaid of the Lord. May it be done to me according to your word."

Mary went to visit her cousin Elizabeth, who was also expecting a baby: John the Baptist.
When Mary greeted Elizabeth, John the Baptist danced for joy inside his mother's womb. Then Elizabeth, filled with the Holy Spirit, understood that the baby Mary was expecting was the Saviour.

She cried out: "Mary, you are blessed among women, and your child is blessed!"
Mary replied joyfully:
"God has done marvels for me!"

On the day of the wedding of Joseph and Mary, there was a big celebration in Nazareth. Joseph knew that Mary was expecting Jesus, the Son of God. He was going to love Mary and protect Jesus like a father.

The country where Mary and Joseph lived was occupied by the Roman army, and everyone had to obey the orders of Emperor Augustus. One day he decided to count all the inhabitants of his empire. Everyone had to go and register their names in the town their family came from.

Joseph and Mary set off for Bethlehem in Judaea, the city of King David. It was a long and tiring journey! But Joseph and Mary looked forward trustingly to the birth of Jesus.

The Angel of the Lord told the shepherds who came running to see the Saviour. They were amazed to see the little baby. The Angels sang: "Glory to God! Joy in heaven and peace on earth!" Mary kept all these things in her heart.

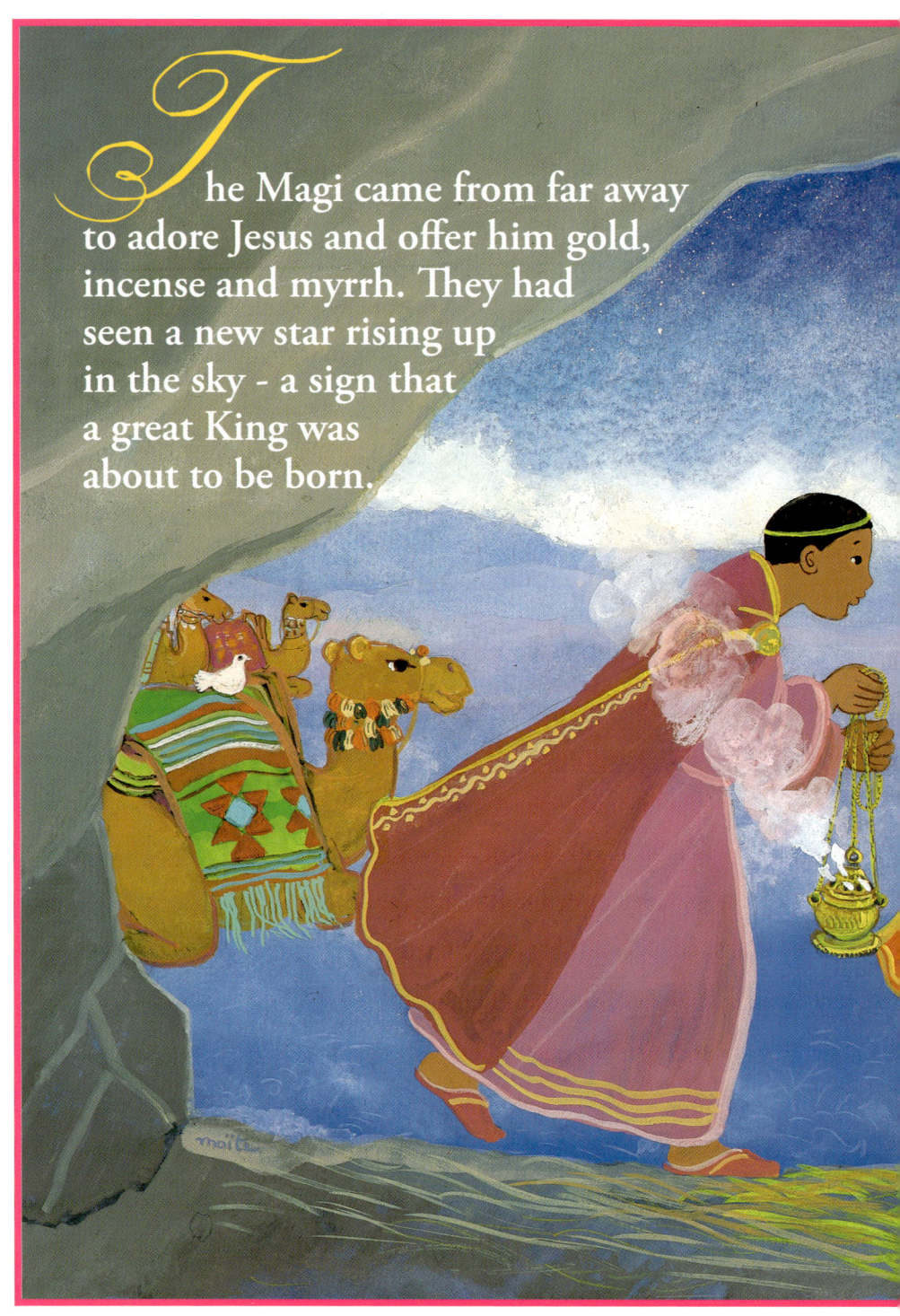

The Magi came from far away to adore Jesus and offer him gold, incense and myrrh. They had seen a new star rising up in the sky - a sign that a great King was about to be born.

Joseph and Mary went to present Jesus in the Temple in Jerusalem.

The wise old Simeon took Jesus in his arms. Through the Holy Spirit, he realised that this little baby was the long-awaited Saviour. Full of joy, he exclaimed: "This is the light that will enlighten all nations!"
Then he said to Mary: "One day you will suffer much in your heart."

Mary and Joseph returned to Nazareth with Jesus. Mary was happy: she spent every day together with Joseph and Jesus. She loved watching him grow. Soon he began to walk! Joseph waited for the day when Jesus was big enough to learn carpentry. Jesus was filled with wisdom and the love of God his Father.

When Jesus was twelve, he stayed for three days in the Temple in Jerusalem with the wise men and priests. On the journey home, Mary was worried: her son was not with the other children.

Joseph and Mary were very anxious, and searched for him high and low. When they found him again Mary asked: "My child, why did you do this to us?"

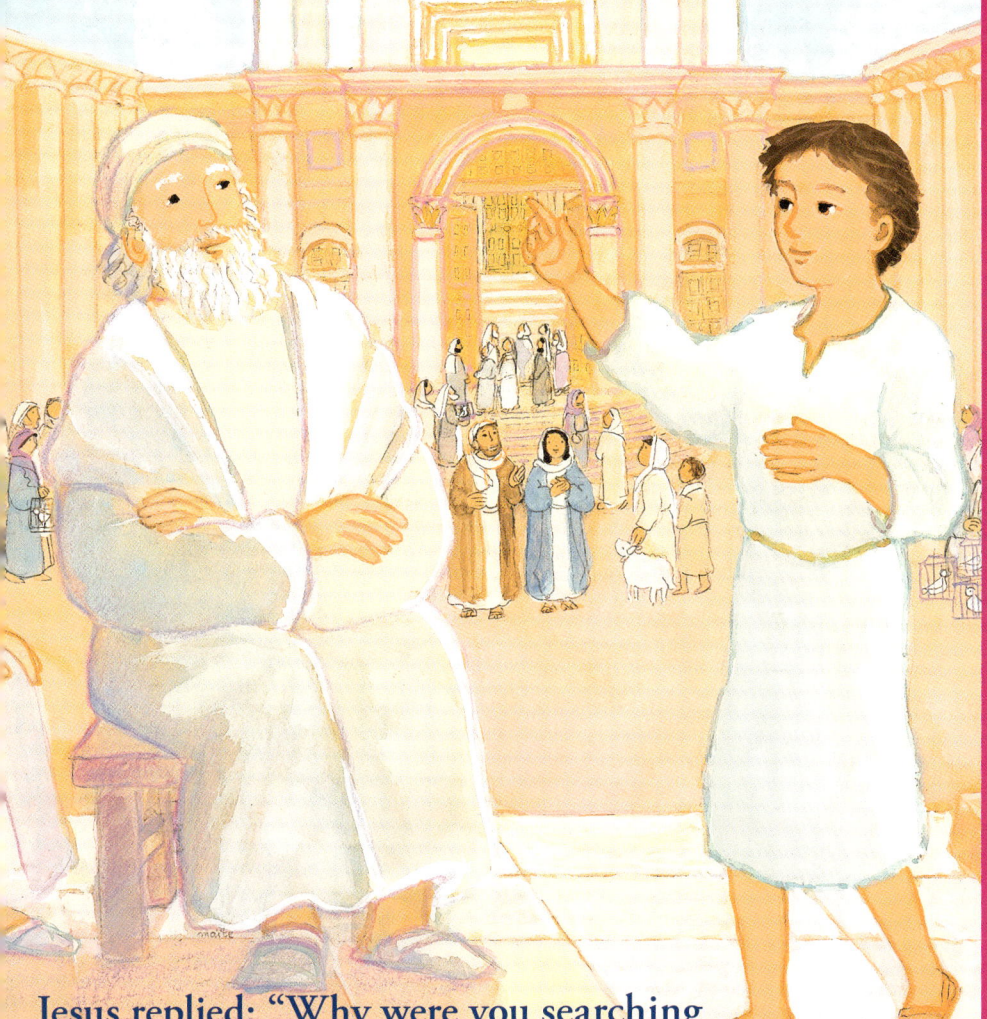

Jesus replied: "Why were you searching for me? My Father's house is where I have to be."

Mary was invited to a wedding with Jesus and his friends. She noticed that the wine had run out, and went to tell Jesus. Then she said to the servants, "Do whatever he tells you."
The servants filled six great jars with water. When they took them to the guests – a miracle had happened! Jesus had turned the water into wine! And it was delicious!

Jesus' friends were astonished, and they believed in him. From that time on, Jesus began to announce the Good News about God's love.

Mary listened to Jesus as he talked about God, his Father. She saw him welcoming poor people and small children, and healing the ones who were sick. Crowds of people followed him and believed in him. But the Temple leaders refused to believe that he was the Son of God. In secret, they promised Judas thirty pieces of silver to have him arrested.

The feast of the Passover was coming. Jesus knew that Judas was going to betray him, but he offered his life because he loved everyone: "There is no greater love than giving your life for your friends."

It was now that Mary remembered Simeon's words: "One day you will suffer much in your heart."

Her son was betrayed by Judas.
Jesus was taken by the priests and roman
soldiers: he was scourged and given
a crown of thorns. He was innocent,
but condemned to die on the cross.

The soldiers nailed Jesus to the cross with two criminals. Jesus said: "Father, forgive them, because they don't know what they're doing."

Mary, John and some women were standing at the foot of the cross. Jesus entrusted John to Mary, saying: "This is your son," and he entrusted Mary to John, saying: "This is your mother."

When evening came, the body of Jesus was taken down from the cross.
Mary and the friends of Jesus were very sad.
They took Jesus' body into a tomb dug out of the rock. A great boulder closed the entrance.

On Easter Sunday, early in the morning, Mary Magdalen, Mary the mother of James, and Salome went to the tomb to embalm the body of Jesus with perfumes and spices. When they arrived, they saw that the entrance to the tomb was open!

An angel of the Lord spoke to them and said:
"Don't be afraid, Jesus is risen, he's not here
any more! Go and tell his disciples!"
Jesus is alive! Alleluia! Alleluia!
Jesus' friends were filled with joy.

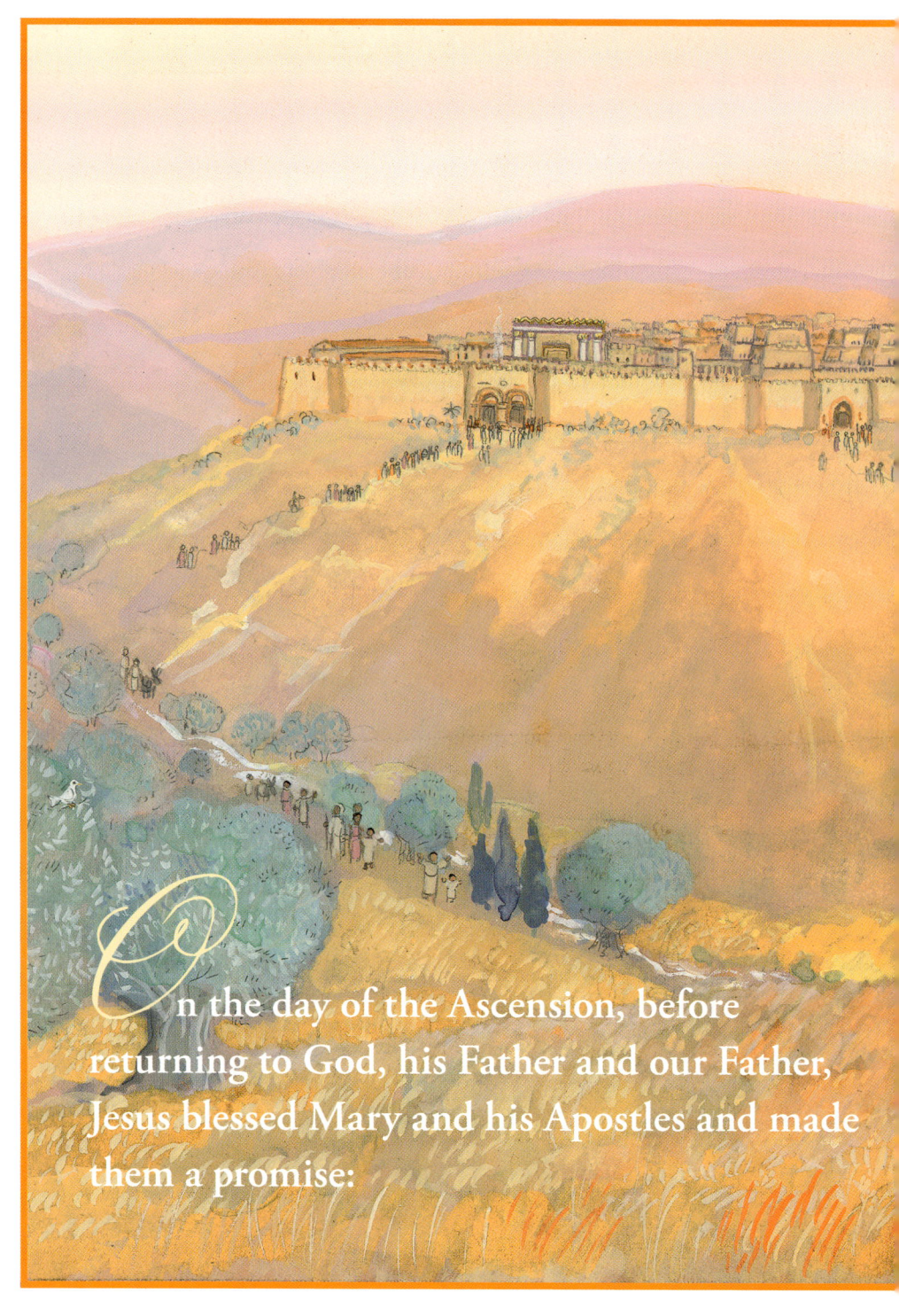

On the day of the Ascension, before returning to God, his Father and our Father, Jesus blessed Mary and his Apostles and made them a promise:

"You are going to receive the strength of the Holy Spirit and you will be my witnesses to the ends of the earth." And Jesus went up to Heaven and disappeared from sight. Then they went back to Jerusalem and every day, they prayed together with one heart, filled with hope.

On the day of Pentecost, the Apostles and Mary were all gathered together. Suddenly there was a violent gust of wind, and something like flames of fire came and rested on them: they were filled with the Holy Spirit.

They went straight out into the streets: "Jesus is truly risen and he gives us his Holy Spirit!" Everyone could understand them, even people who spoke a different language.

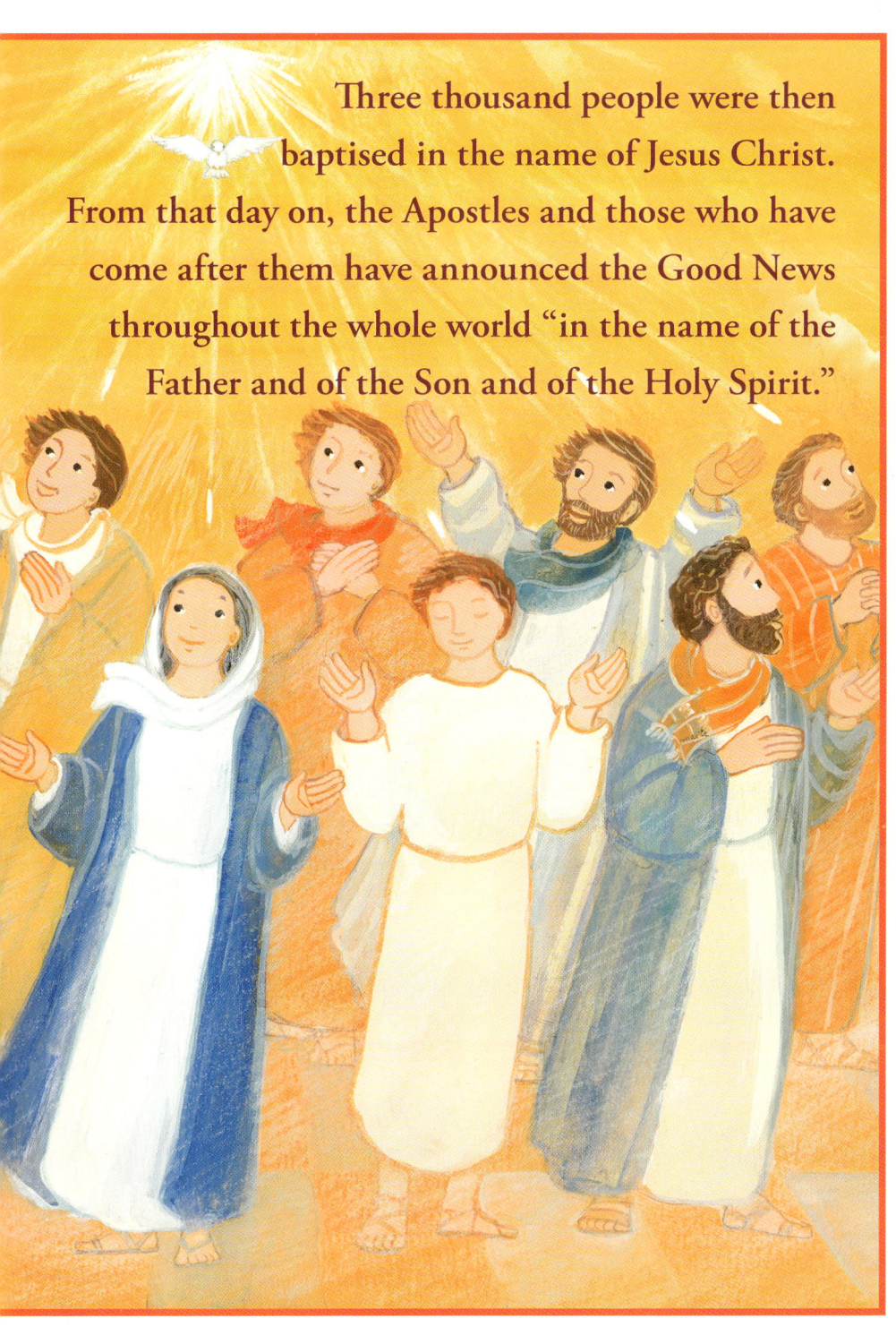

Three thousand people were then baptised in the name of Jesus Christ. From that day on, the Apostles and those who have come after them have announced the Good News throughout the whole world "in the name of the Father and of the Son and of the Holy Spirit."

Having entered into the infinite light and happiness of God's kingdom, Mary watches over each of us as our Mother. She leads us to Jesus in the joy of the Holy Spirit, and brings our prayer to the heart of God our Father. Let's pray to Mary every day, with the whole Church:

"Hail Mary, full of grace,
the Lord is with thee.
Blessed art thou among women,
and blessed is the fruit of thy womb,
Jesus.
Holy Mary, Mother of God,
pray for us sinners,
now and at the hour of our death.
Amen."